THE PUZZLERS BOOK

From the Editors of OWL Magazine

edited by **Elizabeth MacLeod**
illustrated by **Gary Clement**

Greey de Pencier Books

Books from OWL are published by Greey de Pencier Books,
56 The Esplanade, Suite 302, Toronto, Ontario M5E 1A7

OWL and the Owl colophon are trademarks of the Young Naturalist Foundation.
Greey de Pencier is a licensed user of trademarks of the Young Naturalist
Foundation.

This book was published with the generous support of the Canada Council and the
Ontario Arts Council.

Canadian Cataloguing in Publication Data

Main entry under title:

The Puzzlers book
ISBN 0-920775-48-9

1. Ecology – Miscellanea – Juvenile literature.
2. Environmental protection – Citizen participation –
Miscellanea – Juvenile literature.   3. Scientific
recreations – Juvenile literature.   4. Puzzles –
Juvenile literature.   I. MacLeod, Elizabeth.
II. Clement, Gary.   III. Title: OWL Magazine.

QH541.14.P89 1990   j574.5   C90-093762-9

Design Director: Julie Colantonio

Printed in Canada by T.H. Best Printing

BCDEFG

INTRODUCTION

When you hear how pollution is hurting our planet, do you sometimes wonder if there's anything you can do that will make a difference? Here's a book that's packed with ways that you can help. It's also full of puzzles, quizzes and amazing facts about some of the world's most important environments.

Start with a trip to the **CITY**. With so many people living close together, cities often have big garbage problems but in this section you'll find out lots of ways that you can help, no matter where you live.

Then it's off to the **JUNGLE** to discover some incredible plants and animals that make this their home. Did you know that over half the types of flowering plants in the world live here?

Next zoom to the **POLAR** region where survival is really tough. Growth is slow here so it takes this region a long time to recover from environmental crises, like oil spills. Find out what you can do to help.

Take a deep breath and dive into the **OCEAN**. People used to think we could dump any amount of garbage or chemicals into our oceans but now we know that we have to work together to save them.

Then dry off with a safari to the **DESERT**. Although we think of deserts as barren wastelands where very little can grow, there are plants and animals that couldn't survive anywhere else.

Trees in the **FOREST** give us fruit and nuts to eat, wood for building and, most importantly, the oxygen that we breathe. Find out how to help preserve these green giants.

SPACE is your last stop. Discover incredible facts about our planet's atmosphere and what you can do to keep it clean and safe. Find out more about our solar system and space junk too!

Still looking for ideas? Then don't miss the list of organizations and associations that can provide you with more information on whatever aspect of the environment you're especially interested in. By finding out more about our planet and how to keep it clean, you're taking an important step to help preserve all its environments.

CITY WALK

Can you answer these questions and make your way through this maze? Watch out for dead ends!

START

Recycling paper makes more air and water pollution than making paper from trees

YES   **NO**

If you turn off the tap while you're brushing your teeth, you can save about one large pail of water each time.

YES   **NO**

No! Recycling pap[er] makes 60% less a[ir] and water pollution.

Right! You save 9 litres (2 gallons) each time you brush. That means two to three pailfuls a day.

RECYCLING DEPOT

RECYCLE MOBILE

RECYCLE MOBIL[E]

City

WHAT'S YOUR GREEN I.Q.?

Find out how green you are with this environment quiz.

1 The average North American makes enough garbage each year to fill:

a) a bathtub

b) a dumptruck

c) a hot air balloon.

2 Printing all the copies of a large Saturday newspaper uses up:

a) 15 trees

b) 15,000 trees

c) 150,000 trees.

DAILY NEWS
SATURDAY EDITION

3 Recycling is:

a) reusing garbage

b) peddling backwards on a bicycle

c) taping fallen icicles on the roof.

4 You'll find recycled plastic in:

a) paintbrush handles

b) sleeping bag stuffing

c) paved roads.

5 Recycling a bottle saves enough energy to:

a) light a 100-watt bulb for 4 seconds

b) light a 100-watt bulb for 4 minutes

c) light a 100-watt bulb for 4 hours.

6 Hazardous wastes are:

a) a rock band

b) substances that harm the environment

c) a baseball team.

7 Most North American homes make enough hazardous waste each year to:

a) fill a thimble

b) fill a pop bottle

c) fill a kitchen sink.

8 You can reduce hazardous wastes at home by:

a) using natural products

b) plugging all the drains

c) yelling at them.

Answers page 47.

Remember the three R's for fighting pollution: Recyc

6

ENVIRONMENTAL KITCHEN

How many ways of helping the environment can you spot here?

Answers page 47.

euse, Reduce.

MAKE A MAGNIFIER

There are lots of things to see in the city. But to get a really good look, especially at small things, you need your own magnifier. It's easy to make one.

YOU'LL NEED:

- *a small round jar (label removed) with a tight-fitting lid*
- *water*

WHAT TO DO:

1 Slowly fill the jar with water until it's full to the top. Try to make as few bubbles as possible.

2 Carefully add a few more drops of water, then screw the lid onto the jar.

3 Hold your magnifier just above something you want to take a closer look at.

Magnify these:

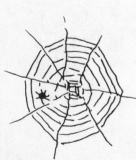

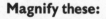
CAN YOU READ THIS?

Special Effects

Move your magnifier sideways or up and down over something. Does it look different?

What happens if you look through your magnifier while you lift it away from what you're looking at?

go shopping, take your own bags to reuse.

WHY RECYCLE?

Every ton of newspaper you recycle saves 19 trees. And recycling saves energy too. For example, it takes 70% less energy to make aluminum from recycled products, such as pop and food cans, than from raw materials.

Jungle Bogglers

1 What is the one thing that tigers have that no other animal has or can have?

2 How far can a cheetah run into a jungle?

3 Two mother monkeys and two daughters went looking for bananas. They each found a bunch of bananas but, even though they didn't eat any, they only had a total of three bunches to bring home. How is this possible?

Jungle

4 Two kids were hiking in a jungle and returned to camp for dinner. One of the kids had a clean face and the other had a very dirty one. But it was the clean-faced one who scrubbed his face, while the dirty one went to dinner as she was. Why?

5 You have an 8-cup canteen and a 3-cup canteen but you can only take 4 cups of water on a jungle safari. How can you measure out 4 cups using only the two canteens?

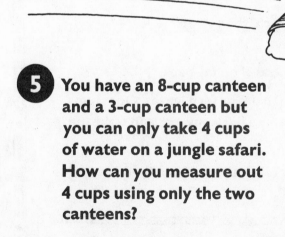

Answers page 47.

JUNGLE JUMBLE

Can you match these animals to their clues, then find them in the picture?

1. We twine our tails together when we huddle in a group to rest.

2. I may look all black, but in bright sunlight you can see I'm really a spotted cat.

3. My tail coils around branches and has a tough pad of skin to help it grip.

4. I'm a slow mover. Green algae grow in my fur and help camouflage me.

5. If a bird pecks at me, I open my wings and flash two big fierce "eyes".

6. I anchor myself to a branch, then stretch out and coil around my prey.

7. My three to five babies travel on my back.

8. I sleep out on the tips of palm or fern leaves. Opossums or snakes that might eat me jiggle my leaf and wake me up so I can escape.

9. My vase of leaves holds rainwater, and snails and tadpoles live in it.

A. Emerald Tree Snake
B. Woolly Opossum
C. Prehensile-tailed Porcupine
D. Io Moth
E. Titi Monkey
F. Sloth
G. Bromeliad
H. Anole Lizard
I. Black Panther

Answers page 47.

IT'S A JUNGLE IN HERE

Jungles cover only about one-sixth of the Earth. However, you'll find two-thirds of all the different species of plants and animals in the world there.

GROW YOUR OWN JUNGLE

Plants grow quickly in the jungle where the soil is rich and moist. Find out how easy it is to grow these jungle and tropical plants.

GINGER

Place an uncut piece
of fresh ginger
in a pot and cover
it with just a little
soil. Water well.

▼

PINEAPPLE

Choose a pineapple with fresh leaves in the
centre of its cluster of leaves. Cut the top off
the pineapple and remove any fruit from it.
Place in sandy soil.

▼

AVOCADO

Avocados with shiny, dark green skins are the easiest to grow. Clean the pit carefully and use toothpicks to support it in a glass of water.

▼

JUNGLE LAYERS

A tropical jungle is divided into three layers. The trees in the top layer, or canopy, may grow to be 30 m (100 ft) high, or as high as about six giraffes standing on each other's heads. Further down is the middle level, then the lower level or understorey. There may also be a few trees that soar above the canopy to 70 m (200 ft), or about 14 "giraffes" high!

PEANUT

Be sure to plant fresh, unroasted peanuts. Watch the leaves fold up at night.

▼

SWEET POTATO ▼

No soil needed! Support the sweet potato in a bowl with stones, making sure to always keep the potato's bottom in water. Choose a potato that has already sprouted, if possible.

Volunteer some time to an organization working to protect our jungles.

15

Bear Necessities

Seals are polar bears' main food. But when bears can't catch seals, they'll eat many other things. However, like you, they do have their favorite things to eat. Each of these three mother polar bears prefers either grasses, berries or fish, and each has a different number of cubs. Can you figure out which mother likes what food and how many cubs she has?

CLUES:

1. Bear 1 likes berries.
2. Bear 2 has three cubs and likes grass.

Many animals' fur or feathers turn white in winter so that the animals can hide in the snow. How many of these animals can you find hiding here?

ARCTIC FOX _____   ARCTIC HARE _____

HARP SEAL PUP _____   LEMMING _____

PTARMIGAN BIRD _____   SNOWY OWL _____

Answers page 47.

Polar

COZY COAT
Scientists think that the long guard hairs in a polar bear's coat are hollow. These hairs carry the sun's energy down to the bear's skin and keep the bear extremely warm.

POLAR EYE POPPERS

1 Can you make this snowy owl catch its prey — using just your eyes? In a brightly lit area, stare at the picture of the snowy owl for 30 seconds or more. Now look at the scene on the right. Do you still see the snowy owl?

2 How much taller is this iceberg than it is wide?

Chilly? Don't turn up the heat; put on a sweater.

3 Which penguin is bigger?

4 How many differences can you spot between these two seals?

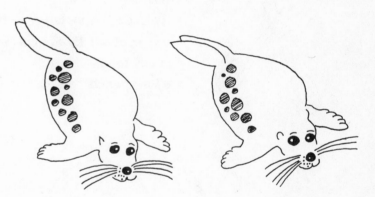

5 What is it?

a)

b)

c)

Answers page 47.

DRAFT FINDER

Brrr! Cold north winds blow down from the North Pole and enter your home through cracks and crevices. These drafts can make you cold and mean that your family uses more energy to keep your house warm. Track down drafts with this handy device.

YOU'LL NEED:

- scissors
- a piece of tissue paper or thin tracing paper, about 15 × 13 cm (5 × 6 in)
- sticky tape
- a long pencil

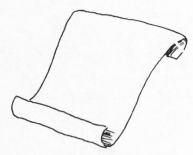

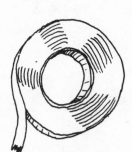

GREEN STUFF

Not only are polar areas cold and dry, they're also very windy. Arctic plants grow low to the ground so the wind won't dry them out, and their roots are near the top of the soil to quickly catch any moisture that falls.

WHAT TO DO:

1 Tape a short end of the paper along the length of the pencil.

2 Test your draft finder by opening the fridge a little and holding your draft finder close to the opening. Does it matter if you hold it near the top or bottom of the fridge?

3 Hold your draft finder near windows, doors, or anywhere you think there's a draft. Once you've located the drafts, see if you can help your parents fix them.

Keep your refrigerator door closed to keep the cold in and save energy.

DESERT DWELLER

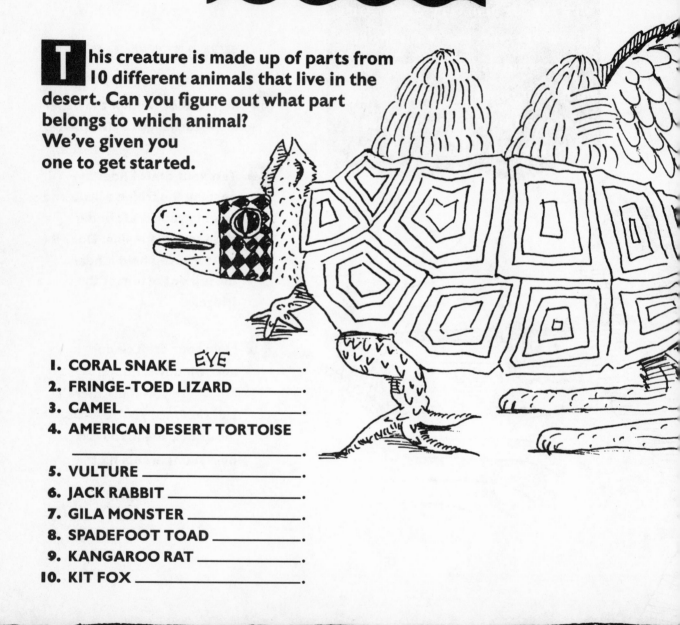

This creature is made up of parts from 10 different animals that live in the desert. Can you figure out what part belongs to which animal? We've given you one to get started.

1. **CORAL SNAKE** _EYE_.
2. **FRINGE-TOED LIZARD** _____.
3. **CAMEL** _____.
4. **AMERICAN DESERT TORTOISE** _____.
5. **VULTURE** _____.
6. **JACK RABBIT** _____.
7. **GILA MONSTER** _____.
8. **SPADEFOOT TOAD** _____.
9. **KANGAROO RAT** _____.
10. **KIT FOX** _____.

If you use an air conditioner, tu

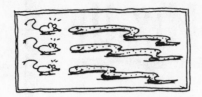

1 If three snakes catch three mice in three minutes, how many snakes will catch 100 mice in 100 minutes?

2 How much sand is in a hole that is 3 m (10 ft) deep?

3 You are hiking overnight into the desert. You're facing north and east is on your right. What is on your back?

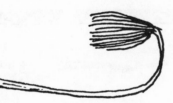

4 What do desert explorers always leave behind them?

5 A girl hiking in the desert placed a mark on a palm tree to show she had been there. If the tree grew 5 cm (2 in) each year, how much higher was the mark when the explorer returned 10 years later?

Answers page 47.

off or down when you're not home.

23

HOT MIX-UP

It's noon on a blazing hot day in a very dry desert and the heat seems to have made some of these animals and plants act rather strangely. How many things can you find wrong with this desert scene?

Answers page 48.

THE ARCTIC DESERT?

Not all deserts are sizzling hot. The Arctic is a desert because it receives less than 25 cm (10 in) of moisture in a year. (St. John's, Nfld. gets over 151 cm (60 in). But the Arctic stays cold, so its snow remains and piles up.

MAKE A MIRAGE

Why can you see mirages in the desert? Find out with this experiment.

YOU'LL NEED:

- *a friend to help*
- *a brick wall that's in the sun*
- *a key*

WHAT TO DO:

1 Have your friend stand next to the wall about 10 m (33 ft) away from you, holding the key.

2 Lean your head against the wall and look down its length towards your friend.

3 Watch carefully while your friend brings the key closer and closer to the wall.

Did the key look "wavy" to you? That's because you're seeing a reflection of the key made by the wall.

How Does It Work?

The air next to the wall is warmer than the air further away, and it acts like a mirror.

In the desert, the air closest to the sand is warmer than the air above it. The warm air bends the light and reflects the sky, making it look like a pool of water in the distance.

If you're dry as a desert, don't run the tap. Keep some cold water in your

Rain Maker

To find out how an Australian native mouse "makes" drinking water, try this experiment.

YOU'LL NEED:

– a large metal spoon

WHAT TO DO:

1 Put the spoon in the freezer.

2 When the spoon is icy cold, take it out and place it on a table.

3 Breathe heavily on the spoon three or four times. Watch the "dew" form on your spoon.

SMART MOUSE

The Australian native mouse lives in the outback where there's little rain or water. To survive, it arranges pebbles near its burrow. These cool during the cold night, then when the sun rises and the air warms up, moisture in the air condenses as dew on the cold stones. Instant water!

How Does It Work?

Your breath is like the warm, moist air on a desert morning. Just like the mouse's cold pebbles, your spoon cools the air around it, and the moisture from the air condenses on your spoon. You've probably seen droplets like this form on a cold drink glass or a water tap on a hot summer day.

DEEP SEA QUIZ

1 Water is how many times "thicker" than air?
 a) 200 times
 b) 800 times
 c) 1400 times

2 Sea water contains small amounts of:
 a) gold
 b) iron
 c) krypton.

3 Plastic bags not only add to the garbage in the ocean but also:
 a) sea turtles mistake them for jellyfish and choke on them
 b) they get caught in ships' propellers
 c) they grow to five times their original size.

4 Tidal waves can travel through water as fast as:
 a) a train
 b) a jet plane
 c) a racing car.

5 Most of the damage to the oceans comes from:
 a) pesticides and chemicals carried from farms and factories
 b) fish
 c) ocean liners.

6 The number of different types of fish living in the ocean is:
 a) 200
 b) 2,000
 c) 20,000.

7 Fish at the bottom of the ocean tend to be:
 a) large-mouthed
 b) big and colorful
 c) rough-skinned and slimy.

8 Because Earth spins towards the east,
 a) water tends to pile up on the west side of oceans
 b) fish swim to the west
 c) west coasts have better sunsets.

Answers page 48.

Ocean

OXYGEN NEEDED!

When chemical fertilizers from farms and gardens are washed into our oceans and lakes, they make the algae there grow incredibly quickly. As they grow, the algae suck the oxygen out of the water and create what scientists call a "dead zone" where fish can't live.

Toxic cleaning products pollute our water. Use natural cleaners like vinegar.

DOWN BELOW

Water deep at the bottom of the ocean is icy cold, much colder than water at the surface. But is the surface water warmer just because it's heated by the sun? Find out with this experiment.

YOU'LL NEED:

- *small bottle*
- *short piece of string (or tongs)*
- *large, colorless glass jar*
- *food coloring*
- *hot and cold water*

WHAT TO DO:

Tie the string around the neck of the small bottle. (Omit if using tongs.)

Fill the large jar with cold water.

Fill the small bottle with hot water and add lots of food coloring to tint it a very deep color.

Using the string or the tongs, lower the small bottle into the large jar. Watch what happens to the colored water.

How Does It Work?

Hot water takes up more room than cold water. The space between the water molecules is greater so hot water is lighter than cold water and it rises. As the hot water cools, you'll notice the colored water mixes with the cold water.

Save water and energy by making sure all hot water taps are turned off.

WATERY CROSSWORD

CLUES

DOWN

1. Some fish hunt in the day, others at _ _ _ _ _ .
2. The Atlantic _ _ _ _ _ .
3. A big, round fish often eaten in sandwiches.
4. Oysters make these.
5. A fish uses its tail and _ _ _ _ to swim.
7. Fish are covered with these.
10. Whales dive deep but must come up for _ _ _ .
11. Groups of fish
13. A baby whale
14. Deep water can be cold _ _ ice.
15. The diving _ _ _ _ _ _ is an insect that eats larvae.
17. They're often made of coral
18. Fastest swimmer
20. Everything
22. Sea otters swim in the ocean but sleep _ _ it.

ACROSS

2. Has eight arms
6. Oceans are blue, gray or _ _ _ _ _ .
8. Some fish hide under these on the ocean's bottom
9. What a diver carries air in
12. A crab grabs things with this.
13. This crustacean walks sideways.
16. The male of these fish carries the babies.
19. Some fish swim slowly, some swim _ _ _ _ .
21. Not closed
22. Either
23. Color of sky and water
24. What heavy things do in water

Answers page 48.

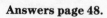

FINNY FARMS

The ocean supplies us with only 1% to 2% of our food but as our population grows, we'll have to rely on the sea more and more. This may mean growing crops underwater or perhaps raising fish the same way farmers raise cattle now.

ELM
- elm trees are narrow at the bottom but they spread out at the top
- the base of the leaf is uneven

MINI-MYSTERY

Getting Ready for Winter

A big black squirrel, a big gray squirrel and a small red squirrel are all preparing for winter. Each has been making a home to sleep in, either in an oak, a maple or an elm tree. And each is burying its favorite food — walnuts, chestnuts or acorns. Look at the picture and read the clues, then try to figure out where each of the three squirrels will sleep and what it will eat.

CLUES:

1. The squirrel that will spend the winter in the maple tree likes chestnuts least.

2. The squirrel that likes chestnuts will sleep in the oak tree.

Answers page 48.

Use the information inside the large leaves to identify oak, elm and maple trees. How many of each can you count in this forest?

Forest

OAK
- oak trees have a full, round shape
- in the fall, look for their acorns

MAPLE
- most maple trees have gray bark
- their fruit have "wings" and are called "maple keys"

FOREST CLEANERS

Mushrooms can't make their own food the way green plants can so they live on dead leaves, fallen trees, etc. This helps keep the forest clean and makes the soil richer.

FOR THE BIRDS

Bird feeders are easy to make and give you a chance to have a good look at forest birds. Be sure to keep your feeder full because birds will depend on it, and place it high enough to be out of reach for cats.

Fill the small tub with feed

make hole here

make hole in tub and lid

MARGARINE TUB FEEDER

You'll need a large, clean margarine tub and its lid, and a small tub for this feeder. Thread a piece of string up through the containers. Use a straw to hold up the large tub.

Red paper flower

Tie to branch

HUMMINGBIRD FEEDER

This feeder is made from a thin plastic tube like those some toothbrushes come in. Make the paper flower red, since hummingbirds like that color best. Fill the tube with a solution of one part sugar to three parts warm water. Stir well.

Cut this side open ▶

Feed goes here

MILK CARTON FEEDER

Use a large, clean milk carton and be sure to include a perch — use a straw or pencil.

When you're camping, be sure to use soaps that don

BIRDSEED PLANTS

Ever wondered what kind of seeds are in the wild bird seed you put out for birds? Find out by growing them.

YOU'LL NEED:

- *wild bird seed*
- *small pots*
- *soil*
- *sticky tape*
- *small plastic bags*

WHAT TO DO:

1 Take a handful of wild bird seed and separate it into the different types of seed.

2 Fill the pots with soil, place a different type of seed in each one, and cover with a little soil. Tape a few of the seeds to the pot so you'll know what kind you've planted there.

3 Water each pot and place them in plastic bags (this will help the seeds sprout). When you see sprouts, remove the plastic bags and keep watering.

Many of these plants are grown as crops for people. To identify your plants, look in a book about farm crop plants. All our crops started as wild plants growing in forests, jungles and prairies. We began growing the more useful plants as crops so that we could grow more of them and harvest them more easily.

SEEDS TO GO

Birds are very useful to plants in helping them spread their seeds around. Some seeds "hitchhike" on birds' feathers or feet, while others are dropped when a bird takes too big a mouthful.

rm the soil or water.

FOREST WORD SEARCH

Can you find all the forest animals hiding here? The wolf has been circled to get you started.

```
R  A  E  B  E
C  E  K  S  D
F  L  O  W  E
E  O  W  G  E
M  M  X  O  R
```

BEAR   **MOLE**   **OWL**   **ELK**
DEER   **MOOSE**   **WOLF**   **FOX**

If you like word searches, why not try making your own?

Recycling paper saves forests! Use both sides before you throw paper away.

MAKE YOUR OWN WORDSEARCH

1 Choose a topic, then write down words that topic makes you think of.

2 Check that your list has short words and long words. Then count the letters in your longest word — that's how many letters across your puzzle square should be.

3 Start filling words into the square, starting with the longest one and working toward the shortest. Check off your words as you use them.

4 Make sure your words move in different directions — up, down, right, left and diagonal. To keep track, draw an arrow beside each word as you use it to show you in what direction you wrote it.

5 Overlap and reuse letters as much as possible. When you've fit in all your words, fill in any blank spaces with whatever letters you like.

THIRSTY LEAVES

In early summer, when a tree is in full leaf, it may lift a ton of water each day from the soil and carry it to its leaves. The leaves use the water to make food for new growth or to make repairs.

SPACE JUNK

Here are some of the thousands of man-made objects that have orbited Earth. Some fell to Earth and burned up, but others are still "space junk." Can you match each with its description and find them all in the illustration?

A. There were dozens of exposed photos on this when it was dropped during a Gemini 10 space walk in 1966.

B. This was the first man-made object to orbit the Sun. The Soviets sent it up in 1959.

C. America's first spacewalker, Ed White, might have had a cold hand after he dropped this.

D. This Soviet space junk orbits between Earth and Venus and sends back data on tiny particles streaming from the Sun.

E. Sent up in 1965, this satellite's shape (like a garbage can) is what keeps it spinning.

F. This was dropped in 1984 during a Solar Max satellite repair mission.

G. Bags of this are regularly tossed out the airlock of the Soviet space station *Mir*.

H. This German space wreck is named with the Greek word for the Sun, and comes closer to the Sun than any other spacecraft.

I. On this satellite you'll find tools, a flag, a photo, golf balls and backpacks.

J. Al Worden let this escape during a spacewalk in 1971 and then he couldn't brush after every meal.

Answers page 48.

1.	Toothbrush	**6.**	Pioneer 6
2.	Luna 1	**7.**	Camera
3.	Garbage	**8.**	Venera 1
4.	Helios 2	**9.**	Glove
5.	Moon	**10.**	Screwdriver

Space

TONS OF JUNK

The total weight of all the man-made objects in orbit around earth is 2.5 million kg (6 million lb), or about the weight of 500 elephants.

Don't ask for a drive—Ride your bike and cut down on air pollution.

ROCKET RACERS

A fast way to do your own space travelling!

YOU'LL NEED:

- *balloon*
- *drinking straw*
- *masking tape*
- *string, about 3 m (10 ft) long*

WHAT TO DO:

1 Cut a piece of straw 5 cm (2 in) long and thread the string through it.

2 Tie each end of the string to furniture (or to two trees outside). Make sure the string is level and tight. Slide the straw to one end of it.

3 Blow up the balloon and hold it tightly closed while you tape it to the straw.

4 Let go of the balloon!

How Does It Work?

As the air in the balloon rushes out, it pushes the balloon in the opposite direction. Rockets fly in the same way.

Try setting up two strings and having races with your friends.

SPEEDY JUNK

There have been 4,000 satellites launched since 1957. About 1,734 continue to orbit Earth but only 350 still work. The rest are all space junk. But they're not just floating around. To stay in orbit around Earth they must be moving at 25 times the speed of the fastest baseball. On dark, clear nights you can see satellites — look for quickly and steadily-moving points of light.

SOLAR QUIZ

How much do you know about the Sun, the center of our universe? Find out in this quiz about the Sun and how it affects our planet.

1 Our sun is: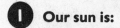

a) the biggest star in the universe

b) the only star known to have planets

c) made of burning marshmallows.

2 The Sun is how many times larger than Earth:

a) 100 times

b) 500 times

c) 1000 times.

3 The Sun makes enough energy in 1 second to supply Earth's energy needs for:

a) 1 year

b) 1000 years

c) 1 million years.

4 How long does light from the Sun take to reach Earth:

a) 8 seconds

b) 8 minutes

c) 8 hours.

5 As well as light, the Sun's rays contain:

a) dangerous ultra-violet radiation

b) pimple-causing particles

c) very tiny turnips.

6 Ozone is:

a) a kind of oxygen

b) Earth's protection against harmful radiation from the Sun

c) what you smell after a thunderstorm.

7 The ozone layer that surrounds earth is being thinned by:

a) chlorofluorocarbons (CFCs)

b) aliens

c) bird sweat.

8 How can you help save the ozone layer?

a) check for leaks in your freezer

b) don't buy things in smooth, shiny packaging

c) write to the government about the problem

Answers page 48.

ROCKET RIDDLERS

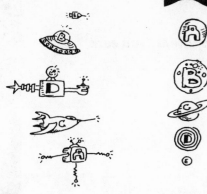

1 Can you get these rockets to their planets without having any of their paths cross?

2 Can you fit the names of the planets into this puzzle? We've put in Jupiter to get you started.

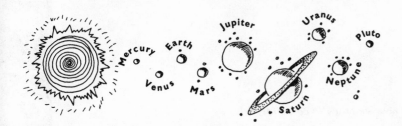

3 Solve these math questions, then fit the numbers into the proper squares in the puzzle. All lines — up, sideways and diagonal — should add up to 15.

A. Planets - suns in our solar system

B. Moons of Earth + planets bigger than Jupiter

C. Hours in a day ÷ sides on a square

D. Days of the week - seasons of the year

E. Planets between Earth and the Sun + sides on a triangle

F. Points on a star + duo

G. Planets beyond Uranus × pair

H. Planets beyond Earth + legs on a tripod

I. Planets between Neptune and Sun - sides on a pentagon

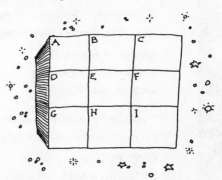

Answers page 48.

YOU CAN HELP

There are lots of ways that you can help the environment. You can:

- *recycle garbage at home or school*
- *raise money for environmental organizations*
- *let people know about environmental problems by giving talks or creating displays at school (or at your library)*
- *write to your local, provincial or federal government to tell them about environmental problems you're worried about.*

If you're concerned about endangered species and where they live, contact:

World Wildlife Fund Canada
60 St. Clair Ave. E., Suite 201
Toronto, Ont. M4T 1N5

To help fight pollution, write to:
The Pollution Probe Foundation
12 Madison Ave.
Toronto, Ont. M5R 2S1

If you're concerned about pets and how well they're cared for, write to:
Canadian Federation of Humane Societies
30 Concourse Gate, Suite 102
Nepean, Ont. K2E 7V7

To get involved with environmental problems like toxic chemicals, energy conservation, etc., contact:

Friends of the Earth
701-251 Laurier Ave. W.
Ottawa, Ont. K1P 5J6

To become a member of OWL Magazine's HOOT Club and get more ideas about helping your environment, contact:

OWL Magazine
56 The Esplanade, Suite 306
Toronto, Ont. M5E 1A7

ANSWERS

WHAT'S YOUR GREEN I.Q.?

1.b, 2.b, 3.a, 4. all, 5.c, 6.b, 7.c, 8.a.

ENVIRONMENTAL KITCHEN

Did you spot: the garbage separated for recycling and the bin for compost (both of these cut down on the amount of garbage produced), glass of water with ice cubes in it, instead of wasting water by running it a long time until it's cold; saving energy by washing dishes by hand, not in the dishwasher, using a phosphate-free detergent, which is safer for the environment; using "human power" instead of electricity to run can openers and knives; dish cloth that can be used many times instead of paper towels which can only be used once; lids on pots to use less water in cooking and cook faster (and so use less energy); mugs with names on them so the same person can give his mug a quick rinse before using instead of wasting hot water to wash it thoroughly; kid saving energy by turning light off as she leaves; groceries in large carton instead of plastic bags; buying food in large, economy sizes which is cheaper and uses less packaging; no fruit or vegetables unnecessarily wrapped in plastic; bread in paper, not plastic; reusable lunch box instead of plastic or paper bag; food in reusable containers instead of plastic wrap, etc; large piece of cheese instead of individually wrapped pieces.

JUNGLE BOGGLERS

1. Tiger cubs.
2. Halfway — after that it's running out of the jungle!
3. The monkeys were a grandmother, her daughter and granddaughter. The daughter was both a daughter and the mother of the granddaughter so although two mothers and two daughters went looking for bananas, there were only three monkeys.
4. Each assumed he or she looked like the other.
5. Fill the 3-cup canteen and pour it into the 8-cup canteen. Repeat so the 8-cup canteen contains six cups. Fill the 3-cup canteen again and pour it into the 8-cup canteen so the large canteen is completely full. That means you have poured two more cups into it and there is one cup left in the 3-cup canteen. Empty the 8-cup canteen, then pour in the one cup. Fill the 3-cup canteen and pour it into the 8-cup canteen which will then contain four cups.

JUNGLE JUMBLE

1.E, 2.I, 3.C, 4.F, 5.D, 6.A, 7.B, 8.H, 9.G

BEAR NECESSITIES

The mom with the three cubs by her side must be bear 2. The bear eating berries must be bear 1, and she has two cubs. Bear 3 then must be the fish eater and the one with one cub.

Did you find the: 2 arctic foxes, 3 seals, 3 ptarmigans, 6 hares, 3 lemmings and 2 owls?

POLAR EYE POPPERS

1. When you stare for a long time at the outline of the owl you stimulate cells in your eye so that you keep "seeing" the owl, even when you look away. The owl you "see" about to catch the arctic hare is called an afterimage.
2. It's as tall as it is wide.
3. They're all the same size.
4. Did you spot: the position of the tail flippers, the number of spots, the shape of the ear, the direction the eyes are looking, the position of the spot on the nose, the number of whiskers on each side, the number of dots on the muzzle.
5. a) polar bear in a snowstorm
   b) fish-eye view of a penguin
   c) arctic fox behind a snowbank

DESERT DWELLER

1. eye, 2. foot, 3. hump,
4. shell, 5. wings, 6. legs,
7. snout (nose and mouth), 8. foot,
9. tail, 10. ears.

DESERT PUZZLERS

1. The same three snakes
2. None!
3. Probably a knapsack.
4. Footprints.
5. The mark would be in the same place since trees grow at their tops.

HOT MIX-UP

Did you spot the: tulips, beaver, maple tree, toucan and tree frog that couldn't survive in desert conditions; the barrel cactus fat and full of water when others are thin and empty; the kangaroo rat and lizard in the full sun when they should be in the shade keeping cool; the scorpion that should be carrying her babies on her back; the occotillo bush covered with leaves (it would drop most of them in the hot sun); snake eating the plant (snakes don't eat plants); wrong trail left by the sidewinder snake.

DEEP SEA QUIZ

1. a) Water is 800 times denser or "thicker" than air which is why you can float in it.
2. Oceans contain all these minerals and many more.
3. a) Plastic bags pose a great danger to sea turtles. Animals also get entangled in discarded fishing nets and lines.
4. b) Tidal waves travel as fast as jet planes which is why they are so devastating.
5. a) Fertilizers and pesticides are washed into the oceans at a dangerous rate.
6. c)
7. a) Food is scarce at the bottom of the ocean so fish there have large mouths that enable them to eat almost anything. Most fish couldn't survive here.
8. a)

WATERY CROSSWORD

Across: 2. octopus, 6. green, 8. rocks, 9. tank, 12. claw, 13. crab, 16. seahorses, 19. fast, 21. open, 22. or, 23. blue, 24. sink.
Down: 1. night, 2. ocean, 3. tuna, 4. pearls, 5. fins, 7. scales, 10. air, 11. schools, 13. calf, 14. as, 15. beetle, 17. reefs, 18. shark, 20. all, 22. on.

GETTING READY FOR WINTER MINI-MYSTERY

You can see the black squirrel is the one in the maple tree. You can also see that the gray squirrel is collecting acorns and since you know the black squirrel doesn't like chestnuts, he must be gathering walnuts. That means the red squirrel must like chestnuts and the second clue tells you that he will sleep in the oak tree. That leaves the elm tree for the gray squirrel who you can see from the picture likes acorns.

There are 2 elm trees, 2 maples and 3 oaks.

SPACE JUNK

1.J, 2.B(still orbiting), 3.G, 4.H(still orbiting), 5.I(still orbiting), 6.E(still orbiting), 7.A, 8.D(still orbiting), 9.C, 10.F.

SOLAR QUIZ

1. b) Our solar system contains: one star (the Sun), nine planets, about 40 moons, 50,000 asteroids and 100,000 comets. And almost all our solar system's weight is in the Sun! 2. c. 3. c. 4. b) Light travels at 500,000 km/sec (186,400 miles/sec) and the Sun is 149,600,000 km (93,000,000 miles) from Earth. 5. a) Ultra-violet radiation is dangerous because it can harm your skin as well as the system in your body that fights viruses and bacteria. 6. all, 7. a) CFCs are chemicals that are used in packaging, in aerosol sprays and in cooling and air-conditioning systems. The government has already passed many laws to cut down on their use.

8. All. Refrigerators, freezers and air conditioners that have small punctures in the cooling coils will slowly leak CFCs into the atmosphere. Have a repair person check yours if possible.

ROCKET RIDDLERS

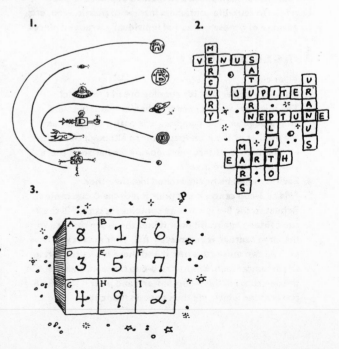